MILE ZERO

MILE ZERO

POEMS BY RYAN W BRADLEY

LIMITED EDITION

_22_ of 25

artistically declined press

o r e g o n

Limited Edition (numbered to 25)
Published by Artistically Declined Press

Cover & Interior Design by Ryan W. Bradley
with special thanks to Steven Seighman

Trade Edition ISBN 978-1-4675-6305-5

Artistically Declined Press
artisticallydeclined@gmail.com
www.artisticallydeclined.net

poems in this collection were previously published in the following publications: *The Oregonian, Third Wednesday, Yippee Magazine, Willows Wept Review, Sir! Magazine, The Northville Review, Oranges & Sardines, YB, WORK, PANK, nibble, This Zine Will Change Your Life, Anemone Sidecar,* and *Big Lucks*

The section, "Aquarium" was published as a chapbook by Thunderclap Press. The section "Mile Zero" was published as a chapbook by Maverick Duck Press.

for Lisa,
always

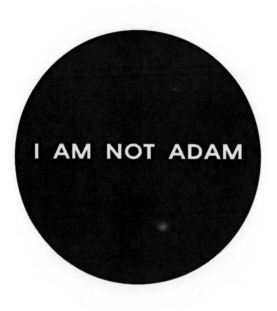

POST-MODERN LOVE

I run my fingers
over your tattoos,
express jealously
at how many more
you have than me.
"I'll slow down," you say,
"so you can catch up."
As if that's not the most romantic
thing a girl could say,
you even agree
to marry me when I ask.

We are one and together
we have twenty-nine tattoos,
so there's no need for envy,
competition, or sacrifice.

Let's turn off the lights,
get naked and forget
whose skin is whose.

IN THE KITCHEN
for Lisa

We make dinner. I grate cheese on the
wooden cutting board, you pull sour cream,
lettuce, refried beans, pico de gallo, and
tortillas from the stainless steel refrigerator.

I sneak up behind you, put my hands
on your hips and kiss your neck. You
pause before plugging in the griddle.

On weekends we eat breakfast together,
I try to find ways to help, pulling
ingredients from the fridge. You
do the real work and I'm rendered stupid,
gazing at you as you move from
the waffles in the toaster to the bacon
on the stove. I could look at you long
past when the bacon will be done.

Let the waffles burn to a crisp.
Let the sausage grow cold. I want you here,
frozen in time in front of me. I want you
as lovely as you are in the morning
when you are still rushing, because it's all you know.
I want you as lovely as you are. It's as simple as that.

YOUR SCARS

Slivers of the moon strike
wildly across your flesh. I
kiss them. Feel the slight
disparity of your otherwise
smooth skin against my lip,
my tongue. In bed in the dark
your body echoes silver slipping
through the shades like the moon
is hiding inside you, amid your
muscles and veins and organs,
housed restlessly behind your ribs.
You're the goddess of the night,
the moon, silver, keeping it chained
inside you for so long. Let them
spill out and I will shelter the pieces
and help you collect them
to rebuild, renew, begin.

ON BECOMING A STEP-FATHER
for Lisa

It's probably for the best that he's older—
grade school age, when I enter his life.
We're playing catch in the backyard and he's
wearing my first mitt. I was his age when my stepdad
took me to pick it out, Ricky Henderson scrawled
across the palm of tan leather.

When I dug the mitt out of my parent's garage
it still smelled of spring, grass, little league.
The sun warms the back of my neck as I show
him how to bring his arm over his shoulder
to release the ball, and his next throw snaps
into the web of my glove twelve feet away.

His light brown hair striking out from under his cap
isn't so different from my blonde. Sometimes I wonder
what it would have been like to have been there
from the beginning. Sometimes I wish
it had been my sperm that fertilized your egg
on some sweaty night. Sometimes I think
this is just right, a man and his son
playing catch before heading in for lunch.

JUNE 5, 2007 1:25 a.m.

She sits straight up in bed, she's misheard me,
waking from a dream where she was getting angry.
"My grandma's dead" I had whispered, still unsure
whether I should wake her or not. But now she's awake
and she's realized she was only dreaming
and I'm forced to repeat what I had said.
"My mom just called" I add, and her eyes are soft,
holding me with more warmth than her arms ever could.

The next day I will stand in front of my grandmother's body
and imagine she is whispering from her pale tightened lips.
It wouldn't be so odd. Part of me hopes she will,
so I can hear her reaction when I tell her I'm married,
so she will know I have a stepson now.

She sits straight up in bed and holds me through the night
because I've learned so much about love
from hearing the words "Grandma's passed" on my voicemail
in the middle of the night. And looking into her eyes
I know even when the world is upside down
we will always be right side up.

THE POETESS IN ME
for Lisa

The poetess in me speaks
in words I don't understand,
like my wife's body—such a mystery,
the way it works, even after she explains
point by point, lying naked in bed,
moving my fingers across her skin
like the best of anatomy lessons.
I wonder if this is what it truly means
to know a woman. That it's not enough
to call it a vagina. Encompassing the labia
and clitoris in one word is wrong,
just like "sex" and "pregnant"
can never explain the particles and atoms
passed between lovers or parents.
There are so many words that mean
more than the receptors firing in my brain
when my fingertips learn what she is teaching.
One day I will write a woman,
and I would not be surprised if it were her.

A WAY TO BEGIN

We got drunk on cheap vodka—
and not a minor drunk,
we smoked Backwoods on the porch
all night, and I don't remember
the moon, or the weather.
There could have been an eclipse
or a tornado and still the only things
I would recall are the words
that spilled from your mouth:
"I'm pregnant" and I held your head
against my chest. We talked in bed
all night, not noticing time until
you had to be up for work. When we woke
I tried to recollect my own words,
lost with so many other details.
You went to work like any other day.
We kissed on your way out the door.
And when you got home I had placed
a rubber duck on your pillow, as a way to begin.

THE FLUTTER OF MY SEED

Moonlight outlines the mound of your belly,
my hand placed gently on the slope,
searching for the flutter of my seed
deep inside. A hint of life slips
across my palm and I am lost beside you,
knowing our child lives in you, feels,
breathes, tastes with you, and soon
we will hold him in tender arms,
love having become new.

FOUR-CHAMBER HEART

"There's something in the heart."
The words come easily from the doctor.
"We want a closer look." The vague air
and dial tone leaves us waiting
for the ultrasound—days of wondering,
of telling ourselves not to research
the possibilities: murmurs, failures,
congenital heart defects. It could be nothing
I remind my wife, myself.

In the grainy black and white
of the ultrasound my son's heart
looks like a four leaf clover.
The four-chamber heart, the technician calls it
as it opens and contracts. I wish
I could see it scientifically,
separate myself somehow, but in turn
it's a clover, the tides of the ocean,
the swishing movement of a squid
seen from the floor of the ocean,
looking up for that last ray of light breaking
the blue-green to call me home to shore.

"I don't see any anomalies," the tech says.
I clutch my wife's hand, watch the sweat
cool on her forehead. I move my hand
to her stomach, feel for the flutter
of my son inside, amazed after so long
to have found a four leaf clover.

WHAT I WILL TEACH MY SON ABOUT BASEBALL

Hate the Yankees.

Root for any team you like,
but not the goddamn Yankees.

No one will ever throw more no-hitters
than Nolan Ryan, it's the only record
that will never be broken.

Steroid users should have been banned,
they've done more harm than Shoeless Joe ever did.

Love is found in the smell of a mitt's leather
and the crack of bat.

But no matter what, when the Yankees win—
even in the preseason, curse them
you'll be a better man for it.

I AM NOT ADAM, NOR AM I BRAVE

I listened to the same album
all day at work

today I searched
"cystic fibrosis"
on the internet

today is the only day
I've wished to be a kid again

I would give a rib to my son
and more, so much more

I would tell Death
his existence is false
and dare him to refute it.

BARE KNUCKLES

In this light my knuckles look soft,
small and uneventful, nothing
like the swollen pink of my father's.

They look harmless, my knuckles,
and the light has nothing to do with it.
My dad's always looked menacing,
gripping a steering wheel or
pulling a belt off by the buckle.

I took a picture of my fist
and stared at it for hours.
Everybody has fists,
but there are differences,
and I want to purge mine
before my child comes into the world
with blank, bare knuckles.
Before my child knows
what a fist is or learns to feel
the bone chips that lie under
the surface of mine and realizes
knuckles don't stay bare for long.

TO LINCOLN

I was smarter at fifteen
than I am now and things I knew
have disappeared except your name
which stuck in my brain
for nearly a decade
and told me you would be a son
before technology could,
which is to say, listen
to your gut and always remember
that love is intuition following
you through years, which is to say,
I'm your father and as such
entitled to all clichés
and to embarrassing you
for longer than you'll find endearing,
which is to say, you're my son,
one of the few things permanent
in this life, which is to say,
you are my world and even though
one day you'll blush
when I say it, I love you.

HITLER KILLED THE MUSTACHE

Not just the loafer fringe he wore,
but the whole spectrum of upper-lip hair growth
was distorted by the führer's misplaced
soul patch. Today someone on TV said
mustaches are in this year and I have
seen a rash of bad ones, from wispy
adolescent moss, to poorly trimmed
retro porn industry carpet swatches.
One day my son might grow a mustache
and I try to imagine the incarnations it might take.
Thinking about these things is like remembering
how cute his baby feet were, until he started walking
and then they were always dirty.

TALKING TO MY SON ABOUT PUBERTY

This summer we've seen the changes,
my wife and I, how his body has filled out,
no longer a stringbean of innocence,
but a young man entering the chasm of puberty.
His nervous energy is constantly channeled
through a fidgeting leg, a flapping hand,
or the stammering of uhhhs between sentences.
My own is focused on finding the right words.

My parents never talked to me about puberty
or sex or growing up, leaving me suspended
in naïveté, but I turned out fine, right?
Still, I can't stand the thought of my boy
going through the torture I felt
during those years, from my peers, myself.

When words don't come, I open my mouth anyway.
One day you'll wake up with hair on your balls, I say,
and that won't be the strangest thing.

PRE-VASECTOMY ODE TO MY TESTICLES

They've been with me a long time.
In fourth grade Paris' little brother
kicked them with cowboy boots.
They were attacked by the backswing
of a 7-iron, and by a flying book
I failed to catch.

My testicles have been maimed
like a dog in a fight with buckshot.
They have been abused—which is not to forget
the tender times, in the hands and mouths
of lovers. But awaiting my vasectomy
the memories that come back are those
that made me sure I was sterile.
Like the grounder that took a bad hop
the day I didn't wear a cup to baseball practice.

They have proven themselves with my son.
Now, I reward them with one last abuse,
taking away what some say is their purpose.
My wife assures me my balls aren't going anywhere,
and the Planned Parenthood pamphlet tells me
I'll still be a man. But I know all that.
Still, I feel they deserve a wake, some celebration
of their existence, their successes and failures.
There's no equating the procedure with the hours
of labor my wife endured, but I've had a long relationship
with my testicles, and it's always uneasy
when the dynamics of a relationship change.

LUCKY

It would be hard to say
I'm not lucky, even thinking
about the doctor standing over me
and my exposed genitals,
shaving me, cutting open
my testicles, and the nurse,
yes, it couldn't just be a doctor
watching my wrinkled skin
shrink from a nonexistent breeze
as they cauterize and sew
back up—sterilized in under an hour.

It would be hard to say
I'm not lucky, even when immobile
for days after the vasectomy,
even after it becomes clear
I'm one of the one in four hundred
left with chronic pain, dull aches
like the lingering cramp
after being kicked in the balls.

I look at my son, now six months old
and all smiles, beginning to taste
words in his mouth, first "mom"
and soon "dad" and the way his eyes
light up when I wake in the morning
and turn over in bed to look at him.
It would be hard to say I'm not lucky.

PINBALLS

The moon is a pinball.

I strangle the beams
that leak through the window.

I set them at your feet.

You are naked
and your breasts
shine like steel.

In the moonlight
I am your pawn.

BLUE THONG

A blue thong lies for days
on the floor of our bedroom.

Tomorrow I will make spaghetti
and after the kids are asleep
we will curl up on the couch.

And, if the baby sleeps
through the night, we will wake
in each other's arms, our naked skin
keeping one another warm.

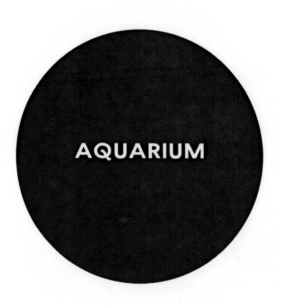

AQUARIUM

EVERYWHERE I LOOK
IS PORNOGRAPHY

I can't show you--
but outside something's happening,
out the window
right now,
it's like an emergency
it's vibrant
it's not at all
like getting drunk with your in-laws
or puking on the lawn
in the morning,
it's more like naked women
in the sunlight, dancing,
but that's not it.

THE TEACHER SAID TITLES SHOULDN'T BE LONGER THAN THE POEMS, AND I WAS LIKE, IS THAT A CHALLENGE?

That's sexy
when you call roll
and I'm tardy.

AQUARIUM

There are things happening,
behind closed doors maybe,
girls jumping
in the cramped space
of public restrooms,
their toes nearly touching
the pockets of their jeans.

There are a million
and one things
I don't know about,
like how a satellite
can put "I Want to Hold Your Hand"
on the radio in my bedroom
or how another
can fire a rocket
half-way across the world,
killing someone
with no radio at all.

And behind the glass
at the aquarium
the fish are surely
hitting on one another,
the girl in tight jeans said,
those bubbles that never
reach the surface
code for let's go to bed,
the twitch of the dorsal fin,
a wink, like every ounce
of innocence I've known.

CHINESE FIRE DRILL

Red lights mean stop,
and everyone scurries
out of the two-door
hatchback, like it's a
clown car at the circus.

The girl, your dream girl
cuts around the trunk,
gunning for the driver's seat.

Two others head that way.

You do a Dukes of Hazard
over the hood and
beat them all.

This will impress her.

Maybe it would,
if it weren't your imagination,
if you weren't stalled
at the passenger side,
watching the others run.

Green lights mean go,
and you can laugh along
with the slamming doors
and shifting of bodies
and gears, even if
you're only a passenger.

THE TIMELESS SUSPENSION
OF WOMEN

there were women in the air, flying,
their bodies suspended with weightlessness,
arms outspread like wings, legs ready to perch.

driving home the same way I always do,
they spanned my windshield, breasts like beacons,
skin flashing like fireflies in my peripherals.

the women were everywhere in the air,
it was one of those days.

THE SMOKE THAT LINGERS

The smoke that lingers
in my lungs,
my veins,
my cerebral
cortex,

clouds my perceptual
awareness
of each breath,
each rushing passage
of blood,

defeats the language
of fire I once spoke
with exhalation,
with conscious
thought
and tapped-out skin,

leaves me
to rub my ribs
together
in the cacophony
of cells dividing
in the hope of recreation.

WHEN I'M SAD I EAT, WHEN I'M HAPPY, TOO

My fingers feel different
on skin than on plastic or wood
or metal or air or on the food
I use like a drug.

THE FAMILY DOG

The elastic crest of sunlight
arced across the bog, crippled
by drought, the alabaster bones
of the family dog revealed
through the cracks of dried mud,
like a reminder that as dinosaurs
once ruled this land, so did Dusty,
a golden retriever with a brain
the size of a T. Rex's and a body
just as forgotten, just as cold.

UNDER THE ICE

I broke the ice with my clubbed hand.
I stood, silent.
The air cracked.
My knuckles swelled shut
      around the black nails
      of water rushing past
      my face.

I let out my breath.
I sunk to the bottom.
My teeth lit up the floor of the lake.
My smile had won me so much,
      every mother said so
      even after I drowned.

COME, LACTATE
IN MY COFFEE

It's dark and bitter
and you could make it
the right shade
of beige brown caramel
you could make it
sweet like your v-neck
collar, you could taste it
and tell me I'll like it
because right now
you know more than me,
you know everything
your finger is stirring
my coffee, you're stirring
my loins and I'm lost
without the caffeine.

NOT UNLIKE MIXED METAPHORS

You think I may be depressed.
In the rear view mirror
my eyes are pink with bloodshot.

I may be mixing memories.

Like the time I drove
five hours to lay with you.

Some days I don't feel alive.

But I dream of your pale body
slipping between sheets
next to my own.

EVERYONE NEEDS A CHEERLEADER

There were two of you
in my dream,
I tried to piece it together,
how you were one
and the same

I saw you in one place
and then another,
I wanted you
to merge before my eyes

but I wanted
you to love me,
both of you

I wanted to feel
enveloped

I wanted it to be
illusion

I wanted it to be
real

so long as you both
rooted for me and not
against.

A SUDDEN SENSATION
EVERYTHING IS TILTING,
A BRIEF MOMENT OF FLIGHT

It starts with your first steps,
but you don't feel it right away,
the world spinning beneath your feet.
But one day you'll be walking,
to the fridge, or maybe to take a piss,
and the ground will feel slanted,
the bookshelves and walls
will be leaning like that tower
in Italy. Perhaps it will happen
at work, just when the days
had started dragging at a primordial pace.
For a brief moment you will be able
to trace the movement of the planet--
that wide, arching swing of orbit,
you will sense the moment,
and you will jump, hoist your feet,
so rooted to the ground. For a moment,
a brief sudden sensation, like an elevator
lifting, will encompass you
with the possibility of human flight.

THE PROMISE OF THE FIXER-UPPER

With a radiator full of rain,
you can sit on the hood,
and catch the stars,
their reflections at least.
You can call it romance
and kiss a girl, your hand
protecting her head
from pressing against the windshield.
You can tell her your ride
will be ready soon,
that you'll take her far away
from all the hometown grease.
When summer's done
you can count on another
coming around the bend,
like a Mustang doing zero
to sixty in a commercial.
You can count on another girl,
whose skirt slides easily
above the knee
and likes the cold steel
touching the underside of her legs,
who will believe in your ability
to restore the old fixer-upper,
and take her someplace
she only names in wishes.
You can tote the stars along.

VALLEY OF SMOKE

We drive
through gray
to get home

we walk
in it to check the mail

we breathe
it into our lungs
and imagine the particles,
like black specks
of cancer

we call our fathers

we say
we are sorry.

OUR PASTEL IMAGINATIONS

We trailed our kites
into the sunset
and its sherbet musk,
and we conquered
the lemon hue
of our mothers' anxieties,
and we grew older,
our feet grounded
in dirt, our heads
rapidly following,
our pastel imaginations
no longer absorbing
or reflecting,
only growing stalagmites
of indifference,
stalactites shrugging
like the shoulders
of our past
unable to make sense
of what we'd become.

I WANT TO BE AN IMPERIALIST, BUT I DON'T HAVE THE LAND

Everything around me
is so large, dominating
my view and my imagination
like breasts on a lonely night
only more political and fatalistic.

STRIPPERS DON'T DANCE TO THE BEATLES

Other girls tuck themselves into the night
listening to "Sexy Sadie" and exploring
the nakedness of desire, the hell hounds
of hope rising in blush over pale skin.

Strippers don't dance to the Beatles,
they save their jar-faces and swollen hearts
for the mirrors tucked in their purses,
only letting loose the hidden purity
of their public bodies for sleep, dreams,
and the dropping of a needle onto vinyl
in the solitude of their one bedroom apartments.

DINNER WITH THE FAMILY

We sit, feral beasts
tearing apart the days,
basking in unheard mutterings
of mother and father
whose breath is laced
with the stink of disappointment.
We are artists, all of us,
whipping into creation
the silence of dementia
creeping over the room,
like spaghetti sauce
spreading over the noodles,
sliding onto the plate
to pool like blood spots
on our brains. We are
a family, each of us
written with precision,
to play a prescribed role
in the devouring of
each other's flesh.

I GET SEASONAL AFFECTED DISORDER IN THE SUMMER

Maybe it's the way
the heat sticks in the cement
and rises through my body,
my organs compressing
and gluing together
in their gelatin skins,
shriveling away
from the bone bars
of my rib cage.

I used to think
it was my blood,
some undefined atom
traversing my veins,
lost, like salmon
running upstream
of my intestinal ruffle,
tainting my brain's ability
to keep things straight.

But how could I blame myself
with disorders being named
like new species? How could I
take credit for anything,
the parasites or myself?

3 BAR BLUES AND
4 PART DISHARMONY

I line up empty wine bottles
on the windowsill,
I take aim with a Lone Ranger pistol
some kid left in the yard

I shoot them down
while the neighbors are singing opera
and jazz and bebop and hallelujah

I line up the bars on my street,
because it's easier to stumble home,
than to take a taxi or fit my keys
in the ignition.

SOCIAL CLASS TELLS ME HOW TO FEEL

I was born poor
and naked, yes
but I had food
and I grew and
was clothed
to keep me
from feeling ashamed.

Sometimes it was cold
in the arctic,
one morning
it was snowing
when I went to work out
and my legs
didn't feel different
even though I jogged
an extra half-mile
that morning
and my scrambled eggs
didn't taste different.

The sun never sets
and digging trenches
is a bitch.

If I was born rich
would it all be
any different?

ALTERNATE REALITIES

Driving the back way
out of town after work
a woman kneels on the sidewalk
next to a white fence

in an alternate reality
I hit her

in an alternate reality
she survives and I visit her
in the hospital

in an alternate reality
she is my wife
and we reconcile
beneath the hospital's
sterile sheets

in an alternate reality
we never meet and I pass her
silently and arrive home
without fanfare to the dog
waiting to be let out
and a dream of a dream
in which we find each other

at last.

HAVE YOU HAD A SEX DREAM ABOUT ME?

I want to hear how you woke,
sweat damp, and trying to place me,
just another man you saw
on the way from Point A to Point B.

I want to hear how you stammer,
slipping, sliding around the subject
with your husband or boyfriend.

I want to hear your eyelids closing,
aching for another minute.

When we run into each other again,
I will see the recognition in your eyes,
placing me at last, and I will hold
the memory of your reddened face
in my pocket for the rest of time,
to pluck out at will, to bask in,
like a mother's milk to a baby.

DEATH IS DRIVING THIS CAR

Oh baby,
you said -- oh baby
death is on your tail
like a license plate,

death is stuck
on you
like tread
on a tire.

Oh baby oh,

I said,
it's your turn
to drive.

AFTER READING, I WANT TO GET DRUNK

After I finish a book I see God.
It makes me want to get drunk,
because I'm tired of him hanging around
my apartment, leaving the cereal out
and watching when I try to get laid

and the way he raises his eyebrows at me
when the book blows me away,
like that's somehow more proof he exists,
when he should be asking how I can question
the muddy footprints he left in the living room
on what used to be an off-white carpet.

MILE ZERO

MY CRANIOMETRY

Three years old, and eager to go anywhere in a car;
you are six, and waiting to put me in my place.
You shout from the back seat for me to hurry,
and I run on little legs, scared to be left behind.

First I hear the creaking of the sliding door being pulled,
then everything speeds up until the van door slides,
wedging my head between it and its dock.

Thwak, the sound of my head being slammed in that door
still scores my dreams.

Now, in our twenties you think we're best friends.
That we've always been best friends;
you seem to forget bending my pudgy fingers back
until they touched my wrist. You seem to forget
slamming my infant head in van doors.

I wonder what kind of damage that did;
would I be a scientist? Did that jar the left brain,
until I turned to the right for comfort?

If I measured my skull it would be one and a half inches
thinner than the average, but one and three fourths inches longer.
At least I imagine this is the only impact
having you as a sister has had.

COLOR BLIND

The paper pulled from the wax,
a mess of gray sticks—
years later I think this is equal
to Sisyphus' boulder: a six year old
forced to draw a man, a house, a tree,
with every combination he can make
out of seven available crayons
because their names have been torn off
and his eyes see only gray.

2ND GRADE
AT BAXTER ELEMENTARY:
ANCHORAGE, ALASKA

In the cold, dark morning of December
we gather and stand at the bus stop,
knowing when school lets out the sky
will be as dark as it is now.

All thoughts are interrupted as we run
across the street to my mother's porch,
chased by a moose who decided
we were too close to her young.

We perch, like sprinters on the block,
ready to flag down the bus when it turns
the corner onto Hampton Street. At school
we line up to enter our classrooms. I linger
at the back of the line, wanting to drop
my body recklessly into the snow
and flap my limbs in scissor movements
creating a blurred impression.

A sixth grader is there, lingering too,
not in wonderment of winter,
but to whitewash my face in the snow,
leaving my cheeks wet, red, and stinging.

SNOWBOOTS

Every winter
we lost boots
in snowdrifts

and moose
tromped through
our backyard

and snow
was a shelf
right outside
the window

and grass
and cement
disappeared

and lawyers
faxed court orders
about which parent
we would spend
christmas with

and the boots
we found them again
in the spring.

THE ARCHIVES OF WINTER

I.

I remember the snow
over the front door
and tunneling out
through the yard
like a prison escape

watching the older kids
disappear into the glacier
between the house
and the street

cars could go nowhere
even if you found them.

II.

We rode in kick-sleds
down the streets of slush
with mom pushing and kicking
and the air fighting
to reach our skin protected
by the armor of down coats
knit hats, gloves, and scarves.

III.

We jumped out of the hayloft
into the snowbanks underneath

our faces stung red
from the cold rush of air

our feet never touched the ground
suspended by the weather
and we climbed the ladder
in the barn again and again.

IV.

Our faces were whitewashed
on the playground by older kids

our faces were whitewashed
outside the house by our sisters

our faces were scraped
by the ice like battle wounds

until the wind hurt like small cuts
turning us inside out.

MARLBORO

My first smoke, passed from your hand,
my sister, daring me to take a drag.
Dad's fingers were nicotine-yellowed
and grandpa dead of cancer.
In a couple weeks you would be living
on the street, but there, on the porch,
you blew smoke in my face,
threatened to tell dad I had smoked,
unless I did for real. I took the pilfered
cigarette between my fingers, stiff,
like tweezers, pinched it between my lips.
I pulled it into my lungs, pretended
every particle was as heavy
as the genetics we shared.

WATCHING DEPARTURES, HONOLULU INTERNATIONAL AIRPORT

I sat, watching the departures,
feeling the panic building
in my throat like an ill-timed cough.
I went to the men's room,
locked myself in a stall.
I avoided the mirrors,
dug in my pocket for the tranquilizer
my sister gave me and placed it
on my tongue, I cupped sink water
in my hand and swallowed the pill.

I watched the departures,
St. Louis, Las Vegas, Atlanta,
London, Rome, Paris.
I thought, what would happen
if I boarded any of these?
What would happen if I never went home?
For a second, a feeling rose in my throat
along with the panic, like hope,
as if starting over could be that easy.

I sat for hours hoping to see
DELAYED next to PORTLAND,
or daring myself to cash in my ticket.

I watched and I sat, then boarded my flight
and wished I was a few months older
so I could order a couple drinks
to loosen the knot in my chest.

Instead, I pretended the tranquilizer
was spreading through my body like cancer,
like the Pacific Ocean stretching out below.

MILE ZERO

The vapor flare cracks like a jet engine
as I break permafrost with a shovel.
Past a two-foot wide trench
the pipeline stretches across arctic plains.

Right now someone is dying over oil,
a million miles away in the Middle East.
Their landscape is not so different from mine.
Seventy million dollars of oil passes me each day,
and there's no reconciling that with dead mothers
and dead children. How can it, when standing feet away
from Mile Zero of the Trans Alaska Pipeline
already alienates me from my own politics?

DISPATCH FROM THE NORTH SLOPE

Every day is a shovel in my hand,
and another trench. Every minute
is a concrete drill twisting
my bum wrist. The alarm clock
is an iron bolt being cut
in my cerebellum. My muscles ache
with the wind's howl. My legs
want to collapse like scaffolding
being torn down. Through summer snow
the pipeline is my spine, wrenching
across the horizon and anguishing
to fail, but sustaining nonetheless.

JUNE 2006 ON THE TRANS ALASKA PIPELINE

The wind is ice—in June no less,
a handkerchief tied around my face
like an outlaw, thinking about
the warmth of the truck's cab,
as I drive my shovel into permafrost,
pushing the rubber of my Xtra Tuffs
into the edge of the spade
breaking frozen ground.

The vapor flare cracks—
brings me back to the shovel,
the dirt, the pipeline, the pump station,
the clack and bump of the bus
to and from camp. Set the alarm
to 3 a.m., work with a bum wrist,
and a crew of men with beards
thicker than the disappointments
they've accumulated. Wear earplugs,
safety glasses, and hard hat. Metabo
blades cut iron bolts, electricians
pull cable, twelve volt pumps
suck ground water from a trench.
A dozer packs dirt, slams its bucket
into earth again and again.
I walk to the break shack
against the wind, cutting
through my hooded sweatshirt
and Carhartts. Seventy million dollars
of oil passes daily, during a war
and a gas crisis, swept under
the rug of the tundra.

XTRA TUFF
with thanks to Joseph Millar

Above the Arctic Circle
blistered, swollen feet
housed in black rubber,
beige accents on the sides
of the foot and over the toe.

Not too many places
do you find so many people
wearing the same footwear.

Steel toes that weigh our feet
like lead to keep us planted
to the earth, as we strike
shovels into dirt and permafrost:

Xtra Tuff boots caked
in rotten diesel-tinged mud
and hardened concrete.

STEVE

Steve the Nazi was my roommate. For six weeks.
Enough time to identify tattoos of swastikas,
SS officers, wizards, and ribbons saying white pride.

The glow in his eyes dimmed between stories
of people he'd stabbed. On the bus
to and from the pump station he listened
to songs about blacks being pimps, crack-heads,
and whores. He said liberals are all gay,
and when we were done in the Middle East
we'd no longer have to deal with Arabs or Jews.

He told me one night he had played Sky Masterson
in a prison production of *Guys and Dolls*.

BIG BANG TIRED

Behind the blackout curtain,
4 a.m. looks like midday.
One pair of socks, then another.
Two shirts, and Carhartt jeans.
Xtra Tuff boots. Get on the bus.
Thirty other men, dressed like me.
Tired like me. ID's checked
at the pump station gate.
Coffee with five sugars.
Into the pickup.
Into the generator building.
Barely able to hold
the concrete drill steady.

In the morning we are tired.
In the afternoon and at night.
Rip Van Winkle tired. Primordial,
Mesozoic, Big Bang tired.
Even when we sleep we do it hard.
Like hitting rebar and feeling your wrist
kink even more. At camp our heads set
into pillows, like concrete in a form.
And they harden the same until the alarm,
and the day starts over.

POST-ARCTIC CULTURE SHOCK

I dare you. Work three months
in a place without trees then go home.

It will hit you, two days later
drinking a tall coffee with your mother.

You will notice all the trees,
and it will make you nauseous.

It's not the trees making you sick.
It's only them becoming new.

FOR THE BIRDS

for Joseph Millar

I was walking and thinking about the arctic,
how we cut the coffee with hot chocolate
and it was still barely drinkable. How some idiot
left the pot on at the end of the day,
and the next morning the break shack was filled
with that bitter burnt smell and sweat,
which had nothing to do with the coffee.
How I was so glad not to be the idiot who had done that,
already tired of being called Commie and Green Peace
because they'd found I was a democrat. I was walking
and drinking coffee, and something wet hit my face.
The sky was clear, I think a bird pissed in my eye.

ATLAS, MISSING EARTH

The weight, now off your shoulders,
your spine uncurled, if not still crooked,
the feeling returning to your hands,
flesh pink and swollen, bitten
by nerve damage and no blood flow.

What else could leave dents
in your shoulder blades, but the
dense groaning earth, the cracked
bleeding dirt, and screaming oceans

what else could this be,
but the distended heart of absence,
the lingering of a phantom limb,
a specter of heft more crushing
than any planet, any orb
the gods could create.

This, you would say,
is the meaning of being lost,
the disorientation of a mother
without child, and nothing would
have you believe otherwise, knowing
no weight could compress your sturdy bones
like that of no weight at all.

PETER SEARS

There's grit in your words,
your voice punctuating perforations
in my brain. There's a parking lot
in my imagination where your poems park
like Buicks. My stepdad's chemo is there
bathed in neon glow next to a Coup De Ville
on cinder blocks. The streetlights are cracking,
blinking, never quite illuminating the message
scrawled in graffiti-hand on the sidewalk.
Your oration is coming across a loudspeaker,
reverberating off the dented hoods of matching Eldorados.
There's a spotlight pointing me to a gray Continental,
I pat my jean pocket for keys—instinctively,
they aren't there, but the doors open easy
so I sit in the driver's seat and lean it back,
let my eyes close and wait for the ether-echo
of your voice to soothe the raging blood flow.

MY MOTHER IS THE ECONOMY

The roof over my mother's bed is caving in,
she brings me coffee at work and tells me
she doesn't want to move into the room
where my grandmother died.

She is out of work, her choices are
to go back to school or find
a way to survive two more years
until she qualifies for social security.

She says she thinks she could work for ten more years.

She says my sister and her three kids
have thirty days to find a new house
or they'll end up homeless.

My mom has diabetes and used to take care
of an old woman until she, like my grandmother,
died in my mother's arms.

MIGRAINE MOON

That harvest yellow tint to my vision,
settled like leaves in my frontal lobe,
rises full and blooms with nausea
taking every turn of my head along,
like a hot air balloon. The unseen wall
of slow-motion universe circling my head,
shattering with each crisp breath.
For a moment, each time it takes me
in its grasp, I know how fragile it is
to be the moon, to slip away,
with the orbit of the world,
so close I can touch it, so far away.

FOR THE LOVE OF WINGS

"Woman swapped kids for bird, detective says"
--*The Mail Tribune*, 2/27/2009

My children, born without wings,
featherless from my womb, pale
and pink and bleating, mouths open
and waiting for something I didn't have to give.

My children, not realizing the existence
of wings on my back, waiting to spread,
waiting to wrap around the young
who needed warmth and flight.

For the love of air, I am a mother,
my launch no longer capable of delay
and what once were my eggs must have
become my golden-beaked heirs, my
sleek-taloned sons and dark-winged daughters
or were returned for the offspring
the sun and moon meant as my partners
to soar with, to taunt the heavens
with our regal aviary performance.

HOUDINI HOLDS HIS BREATH IN THE EAST RIVER

for Jack Driscoll

Your mother called to you beyond the ringing of your ears
from the pressure. The water was cold, but what caught you
by surprise was how her voice contained echoes of a siren song
gargled in the air pockets you sucked for breath.

You imagined staying under water until the surface froze,
scaring children by pushing your face to the glass-like ice
as they skated across your paling cheeks and glacier eyes.

The call of your mother howled, blurring with the pain
of dislocating your wrists slipped from the shackles. You burst
from your trick box, sending a rush of bubbles upward,
but her shrill cries overshadowed the cheers of the crowd,
as if she were awaiting the arrival of a golem.

And as they warmed you with a towel, your shoulders hunched
awaiting the return of color to your gray skin, morbid relief
crept over you, having escaped the call home once more.

ACKNOWLEDGEMENTS

These poems only exist because of numerous influences and inspirations. Original thanks must go to my mother for introducing me to the work of Allen Ginsberg and Langston Hughes at an early age, and to my stepfather for lending me his books of poetry as my reading appetites increased.

To the poetry faculty at Pacific University's MFA in Creative Writing, where I studied fiction, for their willingness to lend me their time and insights. I couldn't be more grateful. Special thanks are due to Marvin Bell, Joseph Millar, Peter Sears, Ellen Bass, and Jack Driscoll.

To the many editors who first published poems in this collection, my eternal appreciation. Especially Amanda Deo at Thunderclap Press and Kendall Bell at Maverick Duck Press, who liked the poems enough to publish chunks of them as chapbooks.

A number of these poems could not exist without my beautiful wife and my two sons, which is just one of many reasons to be thankful for having them in my life.

Ryan W. Bradley has fronted a punk band, done construction in the Arctic Circle, managed an independent children's bookstore, and now designs book covers. He is the author of three chapbooks, a story collection, *Prize Winners* (Artistically Declined Press, 2011) and a novel, *Code for Failure* (Black Coffee Press, 2012). *The Waiting Tide,* a poetry collection written in homage to Pablo Neruda is forthcoming from Concepción Books. He received his MFA from Pacific University and lives in Oregon with his wife and two sons.

CPSIA information can be obtained at www.ICGtesting.com
Printed in the USA
BVOW032136060213

312608BV00001B/5/P